INTERSECTI

LINES

Chris M L Burleigh (signature)

Poems

Chris M L Burleigh

INTERSECTING LINES
Poems
Chris M L Burleigh

This paperback edition First Published in Great Britain
in 2021 by Beercott Books.

Text © Chris M L Burleigh 2020

Design & layout © Beercott Books 2021

ISBN 978-1-9163953-7-4

A catalogue record of this book is available
from the British Library.

Beercott Books
www.beercottbooks.co.uk

To my grandchildren.
May your lives be filled with poetry.

Contents

Impertinence   **81**

Preface

My first poetry collection, Particles of Light, was self-published through Matador in late 2017. My purpose then was to get the best of my poems over several decades into print. I was delighted and humbled to find a readership and I am deeply grateful to all those who choose to buy a personal copy.

This new collection consists of poems written over the last 3 years. Whereas Particles of Light was a collection of private writings, these new poems have been written very much with a readership in mind. I sincerely hope that readers will find even more to enjoy than in the first collection.

My poetry is the poetry of the everyday. Life is often serious, sometimes tragic, but it is also full of joy and playfulness. In all my poetry I try to celebrate Life and to capture my response to how I experience the World whether that is a scene, a situation, or a person. I do not judge or tell the reader how to think or respond. I paint pictures or portraits and let the reader find their own response My aims is always to be good-natured, and generous.

Intersecting Lines is divided into 3 sections – Permanence, Impermanence, and Impertinence, reflecting the living World, the nature of mortality, and humour and wit.

My thanks are very much due to Simon for taking me on as Beercott Books' first poet. My heartfelt thanks go to Judy, Tamsin, Jacinta and the team at Kenilworth Books for believing in me from the beginning and for giving me so much promotion and support. Thanks are similarly due to Warwick Books.

Lastly, I must thank my first and most helpful critic, my wife Margaret, for indulging me and allowing me to write and edit when I could be making myself useful around the home.

PERMANENCE

Black Skies, Black Flag

The wind has dropped
The beach flag has flopped,
Storm sky, churned clouds, heavy hues of grey.

No fun on the sand
No-one in the sea,
No dinghies bobbing,
No windsurfers wobbling,
A cloud-burst has washed surfers and sailors away.

They run to their rooms
They race to the bar,
To drink, to dry, to shelter or shower
Each hoping it will pass, but alas,
No more play, for the rest of today.

Invitation

Bevy of bees
Among the leaves,
An army of workers
Working the blossom,
Lighting, rising, gliding,
Floating over flowers,
A smothered cotoneaster
Weighted in white.
A riot of red berries
A feast for red wing
This winter.

Winter Rowan

December descending
A throng of red-wing,
Thrushes feasting
Frost-ripe berries.
A family, a flock
They flap and they hop,
They stride and they strip,
A ravenous fruit frenzy,
Till all that is left of the tree
Is some leaves,
Then they leave.

Field Pheasant

Field pheasant
Grass-gabled, blade-bathed
Cover concealed.
Red bob head knob
Head bob red knob
Cream puff, blown breast
Cover revealed.
Run, run, hesitate, hasten
Hop, hedge cleared
Drop, disappeared.

Season's Greetings

Fairy-lit pubs and packed parties,
Stoppered bubbly
Ribboned and wrapped.
Contraband chocs
Fine wine and all-trimming dine
Black tie and posh frocks,
It's what it's all about.
Christmas -
What more do you want?

Christmas Shopping

Today I'm going Christmas shopping,
It's such a pleasure buying for others.
I have an idea for each,
I shall bring them all home
Wrap
And give them when I visit.
I'm Christmas shopping today,
I do not want to hear
'We can get it in for you'.
I'm doing my shopping today
Not tomorrow
Not next week.
TODAY I'm going Christmas Shopping.

Migrant Worker

Whistle of lathe turning platters and bowls
Craftsman working far from home,
Leathered hands shining
As he shaves, chisels and pares –
Beautiful objects shaped at his bench.
As he works he tells and retells
His flight from slaughter by a tyrant king,
Of traffickers who took everything.
Among the shavings a small boy sits
Making toys from shapeless off-cuts.
Where they sleep the wife is starting to pack,
Now danger has passed they are going back.
The boy will learn the father's craft
And then one day, by the river Jordan
Reveal himself the Son of Man.

A Drop in the Ocean

We are desperate migrants
Risking everything to be free
We are only a drop in the ocean
War-torn, destitute, crossing the sea,
We are afraid, and so are you
Lost in the sea of humanity,
In truth our numbers are very few
Merely seeking a safe country.

I am only a drop in the ocean
A small boy alone in the sea,
My family longing for dry land –
A small boy, limp on wet sand.

Stockholm Breakfast

Stretch clouds
Sketched on a weak-washed sky
Pallid sun
Warming woken streets.
Sea gulls flapping against whitewashed flats,
Workers walking,
Others stepping to shopping.
Commuter cars gyrating in a basket-weave interchange,
And not every one is a Volvo.

Watery Walk

Tow path strollers
Polished waters
Bank-side ducks side-slide,
Ripple momentarily the silent sheen.

Kingfisher dash-dart,
Air-skip, skim-bounce,
Vibrant flight
Colour rush,
Runs river,
Shoots into shoots
Blink-gone.

Glazed canal
Bowed boughs bowed,
Dripping willow
Sun-glowed, weeping leaf-tunnel.

Slowed, stopped, awed watchers.
A throb of motor heard –
The moment disturbed.

Hard Day's Work

Chilling evening
Sudden click of room thermostat
Shudder and roar of revving boiler
Moans and trembles of washing machine climaxing,
Chime-chime alert, message on mobile
Ping of microwave, ready meal ready.
Grab meal, glass of wine
Sink into sofa
Switch off everything.

Remembrance

One hundred years is long enough for grief,
A tragic time must pass into the past,
Must ease its grip on present and let go.
I cannot grieve for Agincourt,
Do we cry for Crècy
Or weep for Waterloo?
We do not lament the Light Brigade,
Regret Rourke's Drift today.
Soldiers suffered, civilians too,
Families bereaved, breadwinners lost,
History teaches, but Nation sheds no tears
Though once they did –
No-one alive now knew those lives.
Flawed leaders encourage collective grief
It covers their follies and errors,
Excuses for present and future failures.
What madness sent so many to unmarked muddy graves?
History, not leaders, must examine and explain,
And let History record –
Lest we forget.

Give me a Break – General Election 2017

Oh please!
My heart bleeds
When I hear him plead
For a tax break
(For his daughter's sake)
On her school fees.

Taking Care

Startled starling,
Hush baby bird, still,
Caught in my netting
I'm here to help you,
Stay, hold, no flapping,
Spare your spangled new wings.
Fetch the scissors!
There, don't move, snip,
Shush, and one more, snip,
There; free; gone.

Feeding Station

Greedy greenfinches gnawing,
Picking, flicking,
Scruffy goldfinches
Pecking at pieces
Tossing and scattering
Frantic feeding
As if there was none.
There's plenty, you greedy eaters!

Feeding Station (2)

Goldfinch
Bold finch
Feeding with a greenfinch,
Hang-on, hang-in, stay!
Don't let an aggressive greenfinch
Scare you away!

Feeding Station (3)

February fever
Bird food feeder
Greedy greenfinches grab and rip,
Gorging goldfinches tear and strip,
Tits dart and dash
Nip and pick
Peck and poke,
Flick trash, scattering,
Hopping blackbirds scavenging,
Bobbing pigeons ground-pecking,
Birds in bushes poised-hiding,
All to steal, none to share.

Hunted

Spies in the skies
Buzzard in disguise
Winding, coiling
Man-made thermals
Loitering, waiting
Watching, tracking,
Nature's eye-in-sky,
Wide, long, scooped descent
Disappears, distracted by smaller prey
Off-road.

Apology for a Magpie

Magpie, magnificent, majestic
King of crows, regally robed,
Ermine white, bold black,
Shimmering blues, oily greens.
Chattering in trees (so much to crow about),
Such expression (you can't help your accent),
Rightly defending your realm,
Magpie, much maligned,
A warm welcome, always,
To search, and to seek,
To pick and to peek,
To scrabble and scratch –
And to snatch.

Fairy-tale Sky

Unicorn clouds
Mares' tails and manes
White-flicked and flecked on fading sky,
Combed or matted, softly tangled,
Drifting on high breath, else unseen.

Summer Skies

Amazing flight
Majestic Kite,
Slides on air
Glides to nowhere,
Nothing Earth-bound pulls your strings.
Higher still
Hear sharp shrill, a crisp trill,
An unseen skylark sings.
Give me strong Summer days without end!

Written in the Sky

Arabesque clouds
Wisps of calligraphy
Lightly brushed
Gently stroked
On a still sky.
In any script read
'Beauty'.

Skies over St David's Head

Milky Way
Smoked across blue-dark glass,
Pricked by stars
Poked by planets.

Half-moon gold-glowing,
Hesitates, almost slowing,
Heaves itself over a heavy horizon.

Morning moon
Half asleep,
Keeps bleary eye
On the high-tide Deep.

Misty Morning

Pale sky
Weak wash
Yellow glow
Low weeping eye.

Taking a Dip

Slow start
Not-much-morning,
Sun-bed shade
Avoiding burning.
Infinity pool
Muscled water
Rippling light.
Scything swifts
Dip and sip
Dive and fly
Swoop and scoop
Skim as we swim
More wary than they.

Phases of the Moon

Heavy moon heaves,
Encased in cloud
Tangled in trees,
Tries to break free.

A laid-back moon
Reclining on a cushion of cloud.

Annealed moon
Malleable light,
Shield moon
Against the dark blows of night.

A hallowed moon
Half-hidden,
Anchored in a sea
Of jewelled mist,
Impatient, poised.

A lowgold moon
Spying on me,
Nested in a tangled tree
Prisoner in a mesh of branches,
Escapes on passing clouds.

Misty moon
Melting wax
Seeps in tangled trees
And sets.

Fireball moon,
Landed in trees,
Caught in woods,
A forest fire
Put out by rain.

Super moon
Bellied low
On an evening-pale sky.

White
Eyeball moon
Bulging in its black socket
Peering at the dimmed Earth
All night.

Lunatic

Full moon
Wolf moon
Go mad
Run outside
And howl
Forget the neighbours,
They will do the same!

Shopping

Long hair, combed and clipped
Blonde hair, flowing and flicked,
Black raincoat new-stiff and straight,
Hurrying from shop to shop
Worrying from shelf to shelf,
What has placed such pain upon your face,
What strife has put such burden in your life?
And yet you set yourself, and set about,
You work and keep and care;
Stone love, hard-hewn, and cold.
A heart of sorrow for a heart of gold.

The Bookshop

Fenestral figures
Vistas in a glass imaginary,
A menagerie of fables
Coils of dragons
Curled Calibans
Swirls of gold
Spirals of silver
Greens, purples, pinks and royal blues,
Rich verdure of pondweeds
Riverside reeds
Conjured creatures
Water features
Wound, dangling ivy
Tangled trunks
Snails inserted in shaking stems
Floating pictures
Herons and hedgehogs
Tadpoles and bull frogs
Ducks and dragonflies, snails and snakes
Woven into water reeds in willow-shaded lakes
Inverted formulae, flame-fender
Verified Venn-dow,
Cityscape, single spire
Mysteries conspire,
As murals are to walls, all these are to windows,
Writer, illustrator
Poet and painter,

Depictions of plots, moods, characters and themes
Intermingled images suspended in dreams
Inspired by tales
Portals to stories
Windows to worlds.
A world of books within
Taking readers to worlds without.

What a Pain

I have a book about back pain
If a friend has pain I will lend it
But if they fail to return it, then I'll resent it,
I will have to ask for my back book back.
They might resist, and not desist,
And if I insist, they might attack
And if they do, then I'll strike back,
An exchange of blows goes back
And forth, till I stop, turn my back
And walk away. But I'll be back.

Pigeon Fancying

Mr and Mrs
Together in a tree,
What you are up to
Is no mystery.

Running of a roof ridge
Bowing, bobbing, hopping,
All the World watching.
Have you no shame?
Have you no home?
Really, Mr and Mrs Pidge!

Tipping Point

Stuff! Stuff!
I've had enough!
I know what's the matter
I just need to de-clutter.
It brings tears to my eyes
But I know I must downsize,
The shelves are groaning, the cupboards are full
But getting rid is so, so painful,
VHS, cassettes and mini-discs can't be played
They haven't been for at least a decade,
Bedding and towels for a whole family,
They've all gone, and now it's just me,
Clothes so old they're completely out of fashion
But to my eyes they still seem quite modern,
Putting books in the bin
Would seem such a sin,
So what should be the first stop
A charity or second-hand bookshop?
All kinds of memorabilia
Things I'd forgotten as well as the familiar.
A garage full of spares, just in case
Things I'll never need again, but kept because I have the space
Boxes of tiles, off-cuts of wood
Tools I used only once, and ones I barely could.
Do I have a skip
Or take car-loads to the tip?
Oh please help me, take whatever you wish

Really, I'm sure it's only rubbish!
What to ditch and what to save
But I know it won't all fit in the grave

Judge not, Lest...

Hoodied, hunched, and huddled,
Three lads –
Probably harmless.

Taking a Break

Pitter patter
Petal splatter
Battered, beaten
Spring flowers.

Watch at windows
Wait for window
Walk between
April showers.

Autumn Rain

Wonderful!
Regular sound of steady rainfall,
Not intense downpour
Or sudden shower.
Then the silence as it ceases.

Threats

Poor sky
Scowling all day
Trying to smile
Moaning like a child
Wanting a wee,
Late afternoon declares
It's no use
'Can't hold it in any longer,
And it pisses down.

Rain Complain

The rain, the rain!
Philippines typhoon
Destruction of crops and homes,
Mumbai monsoon
Instagram images on mobile phones,
England under triple-rain June
Shots of bedraggled garden gnomes,
And we complain.

Woman in White

Dehumanised, shunted by airport process,
Slow row queued, subdued.

Slim statuette, alabaster face
Stylist-cut, palest blond hair,
Shapeless, sleeveless
Loose summer dress,
Deep-blood, white motif
A flower or leaf.

Eye caught eye,
Anxious eyes,
A cry, a crime,
Travelling alone -
We are all travelling alone.
Somewhere, in another time, another world
I know you,
Impossible, yet certain.

An open mouth
Tongue and teeth
Stretch sticky pink skin,
Burst my dream.
I am shocked into the material,
I pass through the security portal,
You have already faded.

Miss K

Thank you Miss K
For passing my way
For coming together
Like no other.

Goodbye Miss K
You are going away
Our time too brief
Your leaving, my grief.

Open Mic

No tattoos
No piercings
Just a wedding ring.

No hat on bald head
No desire to be dead
No angst, no anger
No seeking danger,
No interminable ramblings
Struggling or scrambling,
No thesaurus thumbing
To find the next rhyming.

Just imagery, metaphor, rhythms and rhymes
Right choice of words
Crafted expression,
And no overrunning my time.

Memorial Bench

An honour, a tribute,
It must have been new once,
Shining varnish, golden laths,
Brass plate gratitude for a life.
Now lichen-clad,
Rotten, soaked,
Re-sited to an uncared corner
Unnoticed, neglected by passers-by,
A seat where no-one now will squat –
I think I'd rather be forgot.

Our Neighbour

The man next door
Is one-hundred-and-more,
When I ask if he's well
He'll say 'Well, I'm here still',
And he still drives his car
To the shops, not far.
His family can't come every day
But I think he rather likes it that way,
He's been here forever
My kind, gentle neighbour.
I'll be sad when I can no more
Say hello to the man next door.

The Price of Happiness

Live in the moment
Go with the flow
Be taken by the flood
Don't swim against the tide.

But moral animals must know,
Values and principles are our lifeblood,
Merely to exist, is to be dissatisfied.

To struggle, to strive
To be content.

Restless

Awake too early
Shy sleep avoiding eye contact
My bed of dawn thoughts
My mind won't lie down
It's up and playing.

A smokey linen light
Stretched on black tapestry
Hanging still, barely creeping,
A room in faint outline.

Wakeful pigeons clearing their throats
Messaging each other in monochrome notes.
So many ideas pressing to be heard
How long should I wait to stir,
To disturb you?

Confession

God comes
In the essence of my wife.
If I have hurt one
I have hurt the other.
As much as I have loved her
I have loved Her.

Music Making

She plays music with backing on her iPad
She makes the music in our pad
On clarinet, sax or flute
She hits the perfect note.
She sings with choirs on Zoom
Virtually filling the spare bedroom.
She plays melody and harmony
Simple duet or complex symphony,
She the low notes and the high
Firm ground, and silk sky,
I the plodding bass clef
Dull though not completely tone-deaf.
As your song soars
I'm yours!

Old Friend

An opened case
A broken string
Your shining face
How we used to sing!
Your bright voice,
Oh my guitar,
My heart, my choice –
We will play no more.

The Sea

Motion and commotion,
Crowded clouds crushing sun
Chameleon light caught in tormented skies.
Wind whistles and weeps
Shudders and shakes
Shrieks and shrills.
Razor rocks, raggèd stack, rising from froth,
Waves crash and lash, wrap and retreat
Hug and hue, ebb and flow,
Seconds fail, then fury flung,
Billow, brew, and boil
A frenzied foaming rage.
Sherds of windspit, splinters of light,
Seeds of a ceaseless ocean.

What's it Like?

Thunder at Four
The forecasters said Five –
Can't they get anything right?
They promised a bright day
But it's just been dull and grey,
And I reckon it will rain all night.

Our House, Our Home

I opened the curtains
I see the decorators have been
A busy night
Sparkle-bright
Brilliant white
Sky a pale emulsion.

Sometimes their taste is brutalist
Concrete grey, industrial fans,
Sometimes plumbers really let you down,
Joints not tightened
Taps left running,
And sometimes the whole ceiling falls in.

But today is perfection
A low-log fire
A warm glow,
And now, inspired imagination
I think the interior designers are here,
Calm, still, subdued mood lighting –
Soft white furnishings and carpet tomorrow?

Black Bat Magic

Dash-bats, flap-bats
Darting high and low.
They shoot and they soar,
They swoop and they scoop.
Are they in the trees or in the eaves?
They come from nowhere,
Are gone, then there once more.
Spontaneous, mysterious
Flight without start, end unseen.
Black scratched on a twilit sky.

All in a Day's Walk

Lockdown country walk, anxious talk.
A ewe waits, her newborn struggles to stand,
Her bloody afterbirth not yet shed,
A scene as timeless as this ridge and furrow land;
Emerald flashing in sunlight, rust red,
Two cock pheasants fighting for a hen;
A fiery fox rolling in long grass
Sunning, preening, away from his den;
All oblivious as we pass.
A line of bluebells shaded in a hedge
Bowing for wildflower addicts' rush.

Heading home, pausing by neighbours' gates,
Showing concern, hearing others' fates –
For her son a mother cried,
A husband tells - his wife has died.
No idyll this, no rural bliss,
No fighting cocks
No brazen fox
No bluebells blowing.
No vaccine in sight
No shield in the fight,
As lockdown loosens, as re-born we venture,
The more we are, lambs to the slaughter.

Staycation 2020

View from my hotel balcony
Views across a wide bay
Glow-sun nesting low after an intense day,
Skating seagulls in flight
Then dead-stop at height,
Shuffling seas scrambling over living rocks
Creeping and fingering into pockets,
Slithering back
Readying for the next attack,
Coasteers leaping into the unknown
Just a few craggy feet below,
Surfacing seals bursting wrinkled sea.
Sipping wine, watching.

Local Lockdown

A holiday maker
Returning from Jamaica
With Coronavirus
(Which he caught from pirates)
Instead of isolating
Went out drinking
Infecting half of Bolton
(Where he'll not be forgotten)
Now he's back in the Caribbean
Never more be seen.

Proofsock

I grow old
I grow old,
I shall wear socks at night,
I'm so cold
I'm so cold.

Falling Asleep

I was drifting, surfing sleep
The closed conservatory glazing
Suppressing sound,
Half here, I heard
Mellow murmurings
And your garden trowel scratch, ring-ping
Scraping stones,
I sensed you were content with your toil,
In and out, rising and falling,
My sleep-breath,
Becalmed, re-assured
It felt safe to let go.

IMPERMANENCE

Killing Time

I thought I had time to kill,
And now I have come to kill Time.
It's been a blast,
Though I knew it couldn't last,
Life's been a breeze
But now I have to leave.
When all is said and done
I'd sooner be here than gone.

The Off

Not long to go,
Got to get ready
But how?
A journey
Or
A stop?
I cannot know –
Best be ready for both.

Quick as a Flash

We have each other as companions,
We find joy in daily interactions,
We each believe that we know best
Our choices better than the rest.
We close our minds and party on,
And in no time, we are here and gone.

Calling Time

Is there really no more time?
I can't believe where Time has gone
I am ashamed how little I've done,
Yesterday seems as today,
And past events as yesterday.
I can't believe Time is at an end,
I can't believe my time has come.

Passing Time

O Time! You are no friend of ours,
You lend us just a few fast years,
You steal each day, you peel each hour,
Brief happiness, sorrow, trials, and tears.

And in old age, in mindless isles,
Or just when we begin to see,
You visit us and rest a while,
Then take us to our destiny.

Ships that pass...

This boat sails still waters
Guided by its crew,
It sails in storms and in sunshine
Then sails out of view.

Letting Go

How shall we say goodbye? In sorrowful dissonance?
Unspoken words say so much more than voices,
Two worlds, an orbed embrace, as silence bonds us.
Shall we laugh at the past, regret all that has passed,
Joys, disappointments, decisions, choices,
Resent what is left, mourn what did not last?
Or gradually, you let loose your grip
As slowly full sup becomes a sip.
We could avoid what's painful altogether
And talk only of the everyday,
Family, news, politics, the weather,
As if there's nothing more profound to say.
No, this is how we'll come to say goodbye –
We'll hug, hold hands, we'll remember, and cry.

A Life

Vividly recalled; vital, always the upbeat,
Every thought her family and her friends,
Remembering each occasion with a card and call,
Organised, organiser, everything ordered,
Nobody forgotten, no-one favoured,
Intelligent scientist, firm in Faith, tutor, exemplar.
Courageous when called, showing the way,
Always loving, always loved; loved always.

Snapshots

A life in snapshots
A flash-bulb, speed of light.
Schoolboy beams
Excessive for the camera.
A wedding pose,
Love composed,
Promises a lifetime future.
Wearied parents, worried smile,
Framed family.
Anniversary contentment.
Milestones, paths trodden, forgotten.
Snapshots of a life
Shutter-speed blink.
A snapshot
Snap shut
A life.

Photo Shop

It brought tears to my eyes,
Old framed photos
A small-town high street
A row of shops
A couple of cars,
Window shoppers
People crossing,
Fixed in one time
Oblivious to impermanence,
I wept, I weep for those passed,
For their past –
The World's indifference.
A person lives and dies.

Saying Goodbye

Such sad times as these,
A mother lost, a child grieves,
A sudden gulf, Life's solid ground is ruptured,
In dark despair all future hope is captured.
Such times, affront to mundane vanities
The world of conflicts, entanglements, and fantasies.
In dazed disbelief and stunned stalling,
Those twilight days between passing and parting.
And when before her bier we bow or kneel
Cold comfort to be told that time will heal.

View Point

When we are gone
No, really, really no more,
When no loved-ones remain
When nobody, no-one can recall,
When others possess our views,
Seas, landscapes, skies,
Who will sense our past presence,
We, stood where they stand
As real as they,
The same joy in untiring Nature?
Who will know
They too must go?

Beyond Important

Even if there is nothing beyond
Nothing is unimportant.

Nothing

If there is nothing,
Nothing is unimportant.

Matters and Anti-Matters

In the end
Not that much
Matters
That much.

Actions

What was done had purpose
Even if there is no Purpose.
What was done
Is undone.
The futility of effort.

Epitaph

Helen Dunsmore
Poet
Died
Aged sixty-four.

Here and Gone

As once he was
He now is not.

Nothing more, Nothing less

We are here
While we are here
And until we are not.
We get whatever we get
And that's our lot.

IMPERTINENCE

Reductio ad Absurdum

Origins of the Universe –
Big Bang
Or
Permanent Firmament.

Neither one thing nor the other

To tell the truth
I am no longer in my youth,
I am an in-betweener,
A bit like being a teenager,
I'm somewhere beyond middle-aged,
But not yet in my dotage.

Holiday

A change
Is as good
As a rest –
I rest my case.

IBS

Three good days in a row,
Not
Three bad days on the trot.

What a mess!

Tit shit sprayed
All across my car.
Pigeon poo
Worse by far!

Incredulous

I can't believe
I could be so naive.

Just Desserts

Dave, Boris, and Jacob R M,
Brexit –
It's an Old Etonian mess.

Take a dip

River swim in Paris –
You must be
In Seine.

Pub Signs (of the times)

Really poor bar service –
Beer with raggèd staff.

Pulled

A bird in the hand
Is worth two in the bar.

Dinner Date?

So, will it be just
Us two,
Or will he be joining
Us too?

How wrong can you be?

An atheist
Can never know
The satisfaction
Of being right.

Looking Back

'Je ne regrette rien' –
Tu es un imbecile.
'I did it my way' –
You have learnt nothing.

Dessert delight

Would I miss the chance
For home-grown raspberries?
What do you take me for –
A raspberry fool?

Time and tide...

Life is a beach -
With rip currents.

View from above

Tall people
Do not realise
How they patronize
Small people –
It's a Little Gnome fact.

Scary thought

The benefits of baldness –
No more hair-raising moments.

A lost cause

Sumatra rhino
'Hanging on by a thread'.

Nothing to worry about

The doctor gave me a terminal diagnosis today –
Oh well, I don't suppose it means the end of the world.

False Falstaff

How subject
We old men are
To the vice
Of dying.

Fame

Fame
Is a fleeting
Game.

A literary life

Shit happens
And crap sells.

The beyond

You'll never know
If there is more
Unless you take the time
To explore.

Retired

Non-workers of the World unite –
You have nothing to lose
But your morning lie-in.

Homage to a Muse

In the spirit
Of Wordsworth
I wandered lonely
As a shroud.

That'll be the Day

That day is one
When we are one,
That day is won,
When we become one.

Just to be clear

A way with words,
Away with words.

Faint heart...

You never know,
She might have said 'yes',
She looked so,
In that ripe dress.

Carpe Diem

Today
Shall I
Take you somewhere
Or
Take you
Somewhere?

This is the Life

I feel so blest
To live a life like this.

History

History is written by the victors,
British history, by the Conservatives.

Deceptive Appearances

Never trust a man
Who is detachably collared,
Especially when it's contrastingly coloured.

Pressing Appointment

Time and Turd
Wait for no man.

Payday Loans

Debt allows you
To buy the future
At the expense of the present.

Not a Sonnet

This sonnet
Is missing some lines
So it isn't.

Vegetative States

I yam
You bean
They worzels.

Chocolate Heaven

Somewhere in a Galaxy
Bar, bar away....

Far Out

You may still be swinging
In your sixties,
But an octagon-arian
Is definitely a square.

Can't Win!

If I don't take the trouble
I'm in trouble;
If I make an attempt
I'm treated with contempt.

Bald Facts

I'm completely relaxed –
Without a hair in this World.

ABOUT THE AUTHOR

Chris M L Burleigh grew up in South London, and read English at Cardiff. He worked in IT. Chris has been writing poetry since his teens, and has been a prizewinner with, and been published by, Fish Publishing. His first collection of poetry, Particles of Light, was published in 2017. Chris is married, with three daughters, and five grandchildren.

Also by the author

Particles of Light: Poems, puns, word play and witty one-liners
ISBN: 9781788039086

Particles of Light: Poems, puns, word play and witty one-liners Abridged for younger readers - with illustrations
ISBN: 9781707237593

Life is serious, but not to be lived too seriously. In this collection the familiar is shown in unfamiliar ways. Our vanity and our fragility are exposed with gentle irony, and generosity of spirit. This is a collection of poems with something for everyone. There is a section on people, places, and Nature, a short section of love poems, and a large section of witty one-liners, puns, and humorous poems.

Reviews for 'Particles of Light'

"This book is both lyrical and beautiful. The poetry is so magical, I just can't get enough!! Definitely recommend to anyone looking for a thought-provoking read!"

"Definitely one of the most 'interesting' poetry collections I've read. Written so differently than anything I've ever seen."

"Through clever use of verbage, the poems become something more, often resembling moving organisms, while others are more like beautifully crafted sculptures."

9 781916 395374